AF264373

Cedar Gets Stuck in Screen Land

Written by
Nikita Paddock

Illustrated by
Tharushi Nanayakkara

I AM RESILIENT. ®
Nikita Paddock
309-1700 Balmoral Ave.
Comox, BC
V9M 2N1
P: (250) 857-5338
E: nikita.paddock9@gmail.com

*For the children of our future,
may you flourish.*

Cedar, the sea lion pup sat in his room and
looked at the clock.
He was bored! It was 3 pm and he knew
that 3 pm was his playtime.

He scooted over to
his closet to find something
FUN to do.

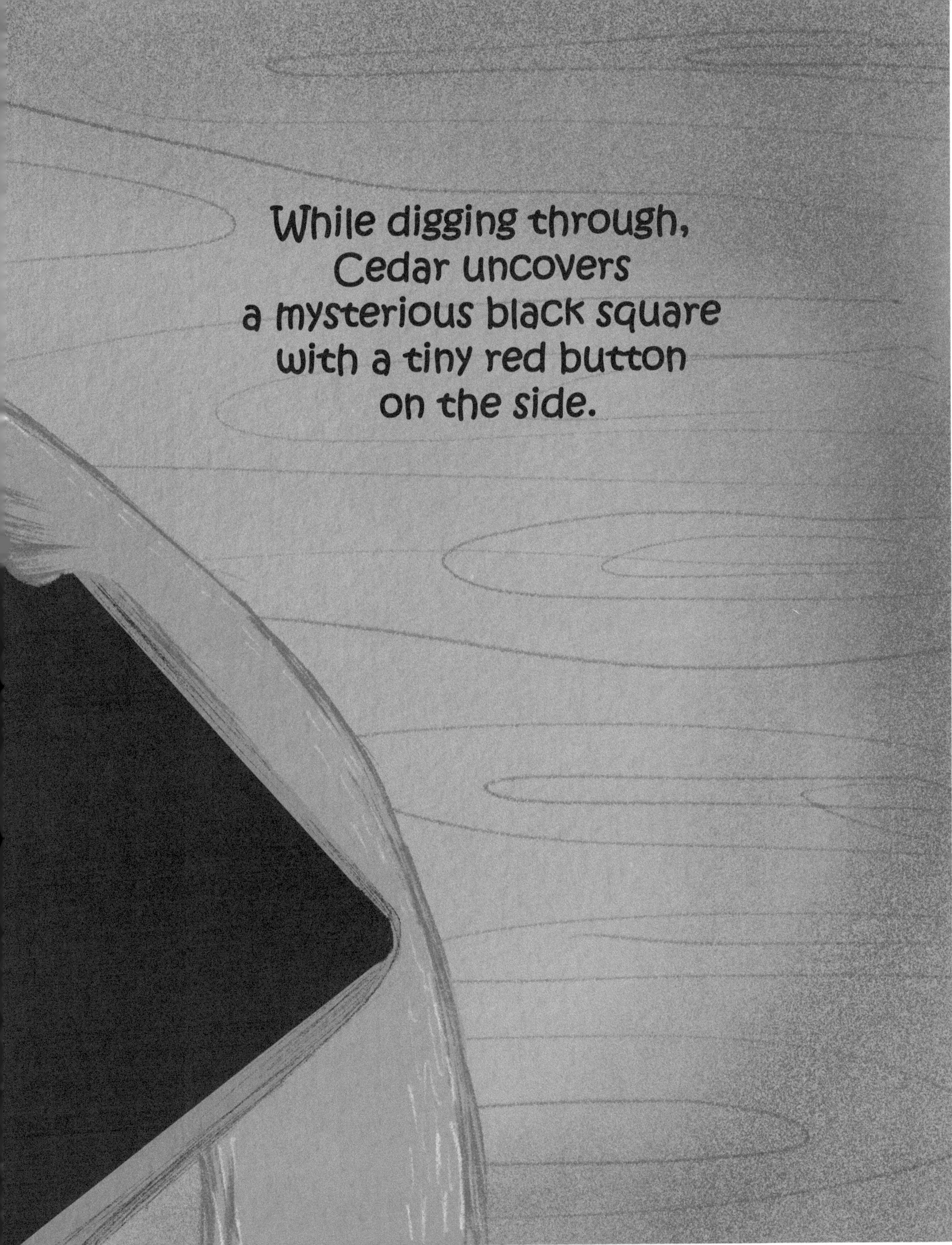
While digging through,
Cedar uncovers
a mysterious black square
with a tiny red button
on the side.

Curious about the device,
he pressed the button and
WHOOOOOSH! He arrived
in the most AMAZING
place, Screen Land!
Games
Ball

Funny
Activities

"WOW" yelled Cedar, as he looked around
at all of the FUN things to do.
This was everything Cedar
had ever dreamed of.
Screen Land had music
he could flap his flippers to.
It was decorated to perfection.
Games beeped and binged and
flashed and buzzed, calling him to play.
"This is THE BEST!" Cedar
thought.

Until... Cedar's stomach let out
a BIG HUGE GROWWWLLL!
I am quite hungry, said Cedar looking
around desperately for a fish snack.
He saw nothing a sea lion pup
like him could eat. While he
continued to search for food,
he missed curling up in mama sea
lion's comforting blubber. "It is awfully
lonely in Screen Land," said Cedar after
realizing Screen Land was not
EVERYTHING he wanted.
"How do I get out of here?"
he honked. Cedar was lost.

Musics
Play

Cedar searched and searched,
and the music only got louder
and lights got brighter.
It was overwhelming
Cedar and he did not know
how to get back to his rock home.

To focus, he closed his eyes
and turned his attention inside.
He planted his flippers
on the seafloor and
focussed on breathing.

All of a sudden, a scent of fish cakes
glided into his nose.
He heard the familiar
clanking of dishes that always
meant mama sea lion was setting
the table for dinner.

As Cedar focussed on the smell
and sound, he even started to drool.
WHOOOOOSH! Cedar was back in
his rock room.

It worked! All of Cedar's efforts to focus brought him right back home. "Cedar! Dinner is ready!" called mama sea lion.

Cedar was relieved.
He expressed to mama sea lion
how glad he was to be home
in their quiet and
love-filled rock home.
After dinner, Cedar snuggled up
with mama sea-lion in their
favourite and most
comfortable rock-ing chair.

Until... WHOOOOSH!